COMPLETE

CRICKET FARMING

PRO GUIDE

A Comprehensive Guide To Sustainable Protein Production, Efficient Insect Breeding, And Profitable Farming Techniques For Eco-Friendly Entrepreneurs

VERN WILSON

Chapter 1
Cricket Farming

Often associated with the sounds of summer evenings, crickets are becoming more well-known for purposes other than their beautiful chirping. They are becoming a vital part of cricket farming, a system of sustainable agriculture and food supply. This technique of raising cockroaches is used for food, feed, and other commercial products. What interests people in cricket farming are its numerous economic and environmental benefits.

Cricket Farmer?

For a variety of compelling reasons, cultivating crickets has become a popular and profitable undertaking for many agricultural amateurs and companies. Crickets are a sustainable source of protein, to start with, being very efficient feed-to-protein converters. The environmental impact of crickets is decreased because they require significantly less feed, water, and space to generate the same amount of protein as traditional animals like cattle.

Furthermore contributing to the promotion of more ecological agricultural methods are crickets' lower greenhouse gas emissions than those of cattle.

Furthermore, a nutrient-dense food source is crickets. Tightly packed with protein, essential amino acids, vitamins (including B12), minerals (like calcium and iron), and healthy fats, they make a helpful addition to diets everywhere. The increasing requirement for healthy and long-lasting protein sources is well addressed by crickets.

Advantages of Cricket Farming

There are other benefits of cricket farming beyond just producing protein sustainably. A key advantage is the great versatility of cricket products. Cockroaches have several uses since they can be ground into flour, powder, or whole insects. For example, using cricket flour in baking, protein bars, and other food products provides classic recipes with more sustainability and nutritional value.

Agricultural production of crickets requires more resources than those of traditional animals. Cockroach cultivation is a viable use of vertical space and reduces land consumption in vertical farming systems.

This characteristic is very beneficial in cities or places with little agricultural acreage, where conventional farming would not be feasible.

A further benefit is that cricket farming has a minimal environmental impact. The much-reduced waste and greenhouse gas emissions generated by crickets than by cattle enable a more sustainable food system. Crickets fed on streams of organic waste can further reduce environmental impact and promote circular economy practices.

Target Market for Cricket Goods

Cricket goods have a wide and varied market potential because of consumers' increasing awareness of sustainability and health benefits.

Cricket goods find a large demand in food. Culinary items that appeal to health-conscious consumers seeking sustainable protein sources include snacks, baked goods, and protein supplements.

And pet food derived from insects is growing in popularity. Crickets offer a naturally occurring, nutrient-dense alternative to traditional pet diets for reptiles, birds, and small mammals.

Furthermore, fertilizers and soil additions derived from crickets are gaining increasing interest in the gardening and agricultural industries. Because cricket frass (waste) contains so many nutrients, it makes a great organic fertilizer that enhances soil quality and plant growth.

Beyond food and farming, the pharmaceutical and cosmetic industries are also adopting products based on crickets. New opportunities for medical applications are being created by the investigation of possible therapeutic properties of cricket extracts, such as antibacterial and anti-inflammatory effects.

Cricket farming offers, finally, a novel and long-lasting way to generate protein and create new goods. With so many benefits and so many commercial opportunities, cricket farming is ideally positioned to make a major contribution to the solutions of the global food security problems and the promotion of a more sustainable future.

To start cricket farming, one needs a full understanding of cricket species, farm layout, supply, and equipment purchase. Since it combines aspects of economics, biology, and agriculture, this project is unique and rewarding for everyone interested in sustainable protein sources and innovative agriculture.

Mostly the species of crickets you have will determine how successful or unsuccessful your cricket farm is. Many species are widely used for cricket farming, each with special characteristics and requirements.

The main species used are the field cricket (Gryllus assimilis) and the house cricket (Acheta domesticus). Because house crickets are typically easier to reproduce and handle, field crickets can offer unique nutritional benefits but may require more specific environmental circumstances. Knowledge of the biology, behavior, and optimal conditions of each species is necessary to develop effective agricultural practices.

Assuring the crickets survive and reproduce in a healthy environment is part of setting up your cricket farm. This covers building appropriate housing, such as cricket skips or containers.

These buildings have to provide enough space, ventilation, and temperature control for the crickets to be healthy and happy. Furthermore, important considerations include illumination for photoperiod control, substrate material (like dirt or coconut coir) for egg laying and nymph development, and moisture levels to prevent dehydration.

A cricket farm's operations are mostly dependent on its suppliers. Scoop and brush cleaning supplies; feeding and watering equipment (food trays, water dispensers); heating and lighting systems (heat lamps, LED lights); humidity control devices (misting systems). It is essential to get excellent, durable equipment that can withstand the demands of continuous use and provide the crickets with a home.

Furthermore, ensuring a morally and sustainably sound approach to cricket farming requires appropriate feed component procurement. Cricket feed often consists of a well-balanced combination of grains (like wheat and corn), protein sources (such as soybean and fish meal), and supplements (such as vitamins and minerals) to meet the nutritional needs of the crickets. To increase the sustainability of your company and draw in environmentally concerned clients, acquire resources locally or organically whenever at all possible.

Successful cricket farming requires not only physical facilities and machinery but also knowledge of feeding schedules, pest management techniques, and biosecurity measures. Raising crickets in the ideal conditions for mating, egg laying, and nymph development is known as breeding.

This could mean providing shelters or platforms for egg laying, and maintaining the right temperature and humidity, to prevent cannibalism.

Feeding crickets should be centered on providing a balanced diet that promotes growth, development, and reproduction. You can prepare your cricket feed blends based on your demands and budget, or there are ready-made ones. It takes close observation of feed consumption, essential dietary ratio adjustments, and access to clean water to manage cricket nutrition.

Since certain insects, such as flies and mites, can harm the health and productivity of the crickets, pest management is another crucial aspect of cricket farming. Among other preventive measures, regular cleaning and the use of natural predators (like predatory mites) can control insect populations without greatly relying on chemical pesticides.

Biosecurity measures must prevent disease introduction and spread inside your cricket farm. This addresses procedures for disinfecting equipment and facilities, quarantine of new cricket stock, and health monitoring of crickets for signs of stress or illness.

Your cricket population can be kept generally healthy and losses can be minimised by early identification and response to disease outbreaks.

a thorough approach to starting cricket farming includes learning about cricket species, setting up a suitable farm environment, purchasing the necessary tools and supplies, implementing sustainable practices, and managing critical components like breeding, feeding, pest control, and biosecurity. By fusing knowledge from business management, biology, and agriculture, prospective cricket farmers may create a lucrative enterprise in sustainable protein production.

Chapter 3
Cricket Lifecycle

The egg stage starts the journey that is the cricket lifecycle, which culminates with the adult stage.

Cricket populations cannot expand or survive without each stage, especially in agricultural settings where crickets are raised for pet and human feed among other purposes.

Care and Hatching of Eggs

Lifecycles of crickets begin with the egg.

The ideal circumstances for female crickets to deposit their eggs are often warm and moist. Incubation is maintaining the right temperature and humidity levels to promote egg development. Artificial incubation methods are widely employed for precise environmental control in cricket farming.

Better hatching success rate and regularity throughout the hatching phase, which this ensures, determine the production efficiency.

During incubation, the eggs develop embryonally, from fertilization to the formation of recognizable cricket nymphs inside. This growth period is affected differently by various species, temperatures, and humidity levels. To prevent fungus growth and ensure the health of developing embryos, the incubation chamber must be kept clean and ventilated enough.

The incubation phase ends and cricket nymphs hatch from the eggs. The hatching process is a critical life-turning moment for young crickets since it marks the beginning of their independent existence. After hatching from the eggs, soft-exoskeleton nymphs grow fast before molting to become adults.

Nymph Stage Growth and Development

When a cricket hatches, it enters the nymph stage of growth and development. Nymphs grow swiftly at this stage as they consume and molt to lose their exoskeletons.

To get bigger, crickets naturally "molt," or remove their old exoskeletons. This cycle of growth and molting occurs several times during the nymph stage, each molt creating a larger and more developed nymph.

Nymphs need a proper environment with access to food, water, and adequate space during this critical time. Cricket farmers usually provide a well-balanced meal high in protein, carbohydrates, vitamins, and minerals to promote optimal growth because healthy growth depends on sufficient nutrition. Temperature, humidity, and cleanliness—all of which also contribute to lower stress-related issues—are mostly responsible for nymph health.

As they go through instars, the developmental stages in between molts, and nymphs change physiologically and take on characteristics of adult cricket.

Development of wings and reproductive organs is one of these, which is required for the following stage of the life cycle.

Adult crickets are defined by sexual development, breeding, and potential collecting for a range of purposes. Adult insects can mat and reproduce because they have fully developed wings and reproductive systems. Maintaining breeding populations and production cycles in farming operations focused on cricket production depends on the adult stage.

Breeding programs for cricket farming aim to increase general output and quality by optimizing genetic variety and reproductive rates. The temperature, humidity, and illumination of regulated breeding facilities are set up to encourage efficient mating and egg-laying. A new generation of crickets is initiated when females lay eggs, therefore finishing the life cycle.

Adult crickets are harvested for their high-protein, nutrient-dense flesh as well as for breeding.

How crickets are harvested will depend on whether they are to be used for pet feed, human food, or both. In cricket production, the need for ethical and sustainable harvesting techniques is emphasized to ensure that the insects are handled as compassionately and stress-free as possible.

In the cricket lifetime, there are, finally, various stages, each with unique requirements and methods.

These lifecycle stages—which go from the egg stage with incubation and hatching to the nymph stage of growth and development to the adult stage with breeding and perhaps harvesting—must be understood to farm and employ crickets.

Chapter 4
Housing And The Environment

In developing a cricket habitat, one must mimic the natural environment while nevertheless optimizing the conditions for the insects' growth and reproduction. Important considerations include ventilation, lighting, humidity and temperature control, substrate composition, size and organization of the habitat, and safety measures.

The extent of your farming operation determines the size of the cricket habitat. A container or enclosure that is at least 12 inches by 12 inches, or in smaller configurations, 12 inches high, can house a colony of crickets. However, larger farming, like commercial enterprises, can call for a certain space with multiple rooms or containers.

There have to be areas in the surroundings for resting, breeding, and feeding. Building ramps or shelves to make use of vertical space can increase available space and provide crickets with multiple levels to live on.

Giving hiding places like cardboard tubes or egg cartons can also help to reduce stress and improve general health.

The kind of substrate has a big impact on the habitat design. Crickets need an egg-laying medium and an absorbent substrate that also provides a surface for molting. Common substrates are peat moss, coconut coir, vermiculite, or mixtures of these. The substrate should be kept moist, but not soggy, for the best humidity levels and to prevent mold growth.

Regulation of humidity and temperature is essential to the growth and health of crickets. Most cricket species do best in temperatures between 80°F and 90°F (27°C and 32°C) most of the year. One can use heat lamps, heating pads, or thermostats to regulate temperatures. Aiming for humidity levels between 50% and 70% will promote healthy molting and prevent dehydration.

Lighting should be considered as well in habitat design. Crickets, being animals of the night, prefer low light during the day. By providing a 12-hour light-dark cycle, normal activity patterns can be promoted and natural environments mimicked.

Ventilation must keep the air quality inside the habitat good and prevent stagnant air. To give enough ventilation, one can utilize vents, fans, or mesh apertures that allow airflow but prevent escape.

Furthermore protecting crickets from predators, pollution, and escape are safety procedures.

Caps or fine mesh screens on containers keep insects out and crickets in. By frequent cleaning and sanitization, illness outbreaks can be prevented and the habitat can be maintained healthy for crickets.

The environment largely determines how well crickets grow and develop. Among these are temperature, humidity, substrate composition, ventilation, and lighting. Farmers can design a habitat for crickets that considers these factors and so maximizes cricket yield.

Environmental Factors for Optimal Growth covers a wide range of aspects that directly affect cricket health, growth rate, and reproductive success in farming environments. Understanding and being able to manage these elements is necessary for a successful and long-lasting cricket farming venture.

Temperature is one of the key environmental factors that significantly influences cricket growth and activity. Ectopics have their body temperature regulated by outside forces. Generally speaking, most cricket species do best in temperatures between 80°F and 90°F (27°C and 32°C). Digestion, metabolism, and general health may be impacted by extremes of temperature.

The use of heating pads, heat lamps, or climate-controlled settings can help to maintain the desired temperature range.

Cricket farming depends critically on humidity conditions, especially during the nymph and molting stages. Crickets need between 50 and 70 percent humidity for best growth, molting, and to prevent dehydration.

In bigger agricultural environments, humidifiers or water misting of the surroundings can both aid in maintaining humidity.

Lighting is one more environmental factor influencing cricket activity and behavior. Being creatures of the night, crickets prefer low light throughout the day. Supplying a light cycle of 12 hours of light and 12 hours of darkness can support normal feeding, mating, and resting habits and mimic natural settings.

Ventilation is necessary to keep the cricket habitat air-quality-maintained and to prevent moisture, odors, and gas collection. To give enough ventilation, one can utilize vents, fans, or mesh apertures that allow airflow but prevent escape.

One environmental factor directly influencing cricket reproduction and health is the composition of the substrate. An absorbent substrate should also provide a surface for molting and a place to lay eggs.

Typical substrates are peat moss, coconut coir, vermiculite, or mixtures of these. The substrate should be kept moist but not soggy for the ideal humidity levels and to prevent mold growth.

Control of pests and diseases is an essential part of environmental management in cricket production. Routine inspection of insects, flies, and parasites to prevent infestations that could harm cricket populations, is necessary.

Using predatory mites and other naturally occurring predators, organic pest management methods can help manage pest populations without putting insects or the environment at risk.

All things considered, controlling temperature, humidity, lighting, substrate composition, ventilation, and pest control is necessary to promote optimal growth, health, and productivity in cricket farming operations. Farmers who are aware of and in charge of these factors can give their cricket colonies a healthy and long-lasting habitat.

Pest and disease management in cricket farming includes the identification, control, and prevention of diseases and pests that may impact the populations of crickets and overall farm output. It takes efficient pest and disease management plans to maintain a healthy and sustainable cricket farming operation.

Cockroaches, flies, ants, and mites are among the typical pests that might infest cricket colonies. Diseases can proliferate, resources contested, and cricket habitats destroyed by these insects. Continual observation and early detection of infestations are crucial elements of pest management. Visual checks, sticky traps, and monitoring equipment can all be helpful before bug numbers become a major problem.

Integrated pest management (IPM) techniques can reduce environmental impact while also providing effective pest control. Maintaining habitats clean and hygienic, removing waste, and reducing potential pest areas are some cultural practices that may be incorporated into IPM techniques.

Barriers and traps are two other mechanical treatments that help reduce pest populations.

Biological management methods try to lower pest populations by the use of parasites or natural predators. Predatory mites, for example, can be placed into cricket homes to control mite infestations without affecting crickets. In a similar line, fly populations can be controlled by parasitic wasps.

Chemical control methods need to be used carefully and only as a last resort to avoid harming insects, people, or the environment. Should chemical treatments be necessary, it is advisable to apply focused, low-toxicity pesticides. Chemical controls have to be applied correctly and with safety precautions taken.

Disease management is another essential part of pest and disease control in cricket farming. Common illnesses that can strike cockroaches include bacterial, fungal, and viral ones. Disease epidemics are prevented in part by isolating sick or infected individuals, maintaining sanitary and clean surroundings, and implementing biosecurity measures.

Continually watching cricket populations for signs of illness or abnormal behavior can help with early diagnosis and treatment of disease issues. Ask a veterinarian or experienced entomologist for guidance on disease diagnosis and treatment regimens.

Effective control of insects and diseases in cricket farming requires a proactive approach that emphasizes prevention, integrates numerous control methods, and lessens environmental impact. Good methods of pest and disease control allow farmers to protect their

Chapter 5
Feeding And Nutrition

The success of cricket farming for personal, pet, or commercial feed primarily depends on nutrition and feeding. Knowing the finer aspects of cricket diet requirements, effective feeding methods, and the use of nutritional supplements and various feed sources are essential to maintaining healthy cricket farming practices.

Must Haves for a Cricket Diet

For the best possible life and development, crickets need specific nutrients, just like any other living thing. Their development, reproduction, and overall health depend on a diet high in many nutrients.

A cricket eats mostly protein. Proteins are essential to the growth of muscles, tissue repair, hormone and enzyme synthesis, and other functions of the cricket.

Crickets require carbohydrates as well as proteins for energy.

The primary fuel, carbohydrates provide the energy needed for growth, mobility, and several physiological processes.

A further necessary diet for crickets is fiber, which aids in digestion and supports gut health.

Crickets need proteins, carbohydrates, and fiber in addition to vitamins and minerals to maintain their health. Vitamins A, B complex, C, D, and E are essential to many metabolic functions, immune system function, and overall growth. Additionally necessary for muscle contraction, electrolyte balance, and bone formation are minerals like calcium, phosphorus, potassium, magnesium, and iron.

Techniques for Effective Feeding

Effective feeding methods are essential to crickets' maximum development, reproduction rates, and general output. Providing a well-balanced diet that meets every nutritional requirement of crickets is one such method.

This gives a variety of feed sources in the right proportions of proteins, carbohydrates, fibers, vitamins, and minerals.

The frequency and quantity of feeding to the crickets have a significant impact on feeding efficiency as well. It is necessary to follow a regular feeding schedule to ensure crickets always have food accessible.

Cricket health and growth may suffer from both excessive and insufficient eating. The best outcomes depend on feeding methods being changed in reaction to feed intake monitoring.

Apart from that, proper feed management must prevent waste and contamination. Feeds should be kept in dry, hygienic locations with adequate ventilation to prevent mold and decay. Feeders designed to minimize waste and spills are another way that feeding efficiency and economy are increased.

Nutritional supplements can help crickets get more from their primary diet and be in better general condition. Probiotics, calcium powder, vitamin supplements, and growth promoters can be added to their food to deal with specific nutritional deficiencies or enhance performance.

Crickets can get food from several sources. One popular feed source is commercial cricket feed, which is designed specifically to meet cricket's nutritional needs. Many times, these meals provide a well-balanced mix of proteins, carbohydrates, vitamins, and minerals that are essential for cricket's health.

Apart from commercial meals, crickets can consume a wide range of organic substances. This includes grains like wheat, corn, and oats as well as fruit and vegetables like apples, carrots, and leafy greens. Using organic waste products like food scraps or agricultural byproducts is another cost- and environmentally-friendly way to feed crickets.

Mealworms, larvae of black army flies, or fish meal can also provide added nutrition and variety to cricket diets. Cricket feed can have its nutritional composition improved and proper development encouraged by the use of these high-protein additions.

successful cricket farming needs an understanding of the requirements of the cricket diet, efficient feeding methods, and the utilization of various feed sources and nutritional supplements.

Giving nutrition and feed management first attention will help farmers ensure the health, productivity, and sustainability of their cricket colonies for a variety of purposes.

Chapter 6
The Breeding And Reproduction

Breeding and reproduction are basic elements of cricket farming that have an immediate impact on the viability and sustainability of the operation. One has to know cricket mating behavior to reproduce effectively; optimal practices and appropriate breeding techniques ensure the best results. Taking care of the egg-laying and hatchling care also promotes the growth and flourishing of a healthy cricket population.

Cricket mating behavior is intricate and necessary for successful reproduction. Mostly, the well-known chirping of crickets is a male mating sound meant to attract females. Understanding these signals is essential for farmers to identify mating pairings and facilitate the breeding process. Male crickets make sounds that differ among species and indicate when they are ready to mate by rubbing their wings together. Mating interactions arise when females approach males in answer to these calls.

Breeding techniques and best practices determine how well cricket farms reproduce. One widely used method is to use enclosures or chambers made to seem like suitable mating habitats in nature. Sometimes these chambers include substrate materials like dirt or sand that provide the perfect environment for egg laying. To encourage mating behavior and increase the likelihood of successful reproduction, farmers may add specific environmental elements, such as temperature and humidity.

The control of egg-laying and hatchling care determines the life and growth of the cricket population. Female crickets typically deposit their eggs in groups in certain areas of the mating chamber, the substrate. Watching these egg deposits, farmers take precautions to protect them from the weather and predators. Hatchlings are ensured the highest possible air quality via sufficient ventilation, while humidity levels are maintained constant to prevent egg desiccation.

Providing nymphs with a healthy environment to grow is part of hatchling care. Farmers can separate the juveniles and adults of crickets to avoid cannibalism and to provide enough food and water. The quick growth of hatchlings could require dietary supplements to ensure their early maturity. Farmers track growing rates and general health measures to assess how well their breeding and reproduction strategies are working.

All things considered, breeding and reproduction in cricket farming require a deep understanding of mating behavior, effective breeding techniques, and meticulous egg-laying and hatchling care. By optimizing these aspects, farms may profitably and successfully raise the number of crickets.

Harvesting and processing crickets is an essential part of cricket farming; it requires close attention to detail and morality. The best crickets for processing are guaranteed when you harvest at the right time, and ethical agricultural practices depend on using humane harvesting methods. The way crickets are cleaned, processed, and packaged also has a significant impact on producing safe and high-quality finished cricket products.

When to Harvest

The finest potential condition for processing crickets will be ensured if you harvest them at the appropriate time. Generally speaking, crickets are gathered when they reach the proper size and maturity to be consumed or further processed into products. When the harvest occurs can depend on the planned use of the crickets—human consumption, pet feed, or agricultural application.

Two key indicators of when is best to gather crickets are their age and developmental stage. When crickets are adults but before their life cycle ends, for example, you could want to gather them for human consumption. This ensures that the crickets keep theirness and good nutritional balance.

Planning your harvest should consider the cause of the crickets. For instance, you might want to collect crickets at a somewhat different stage than you would if you were collecting them for pet food. This is so because different animals may have different nutritional requirements and the ideal stage of cricket development for pet feed may not be the same as that for human consumption.

Categories of Humane Harvesting

For cricket farming to maintain moral farming methods and ensure the health of the crickets, humane harvesting methods are essential. Many kind harvesting methods are available to farmers to lessen the stress and suffering of the crickets throughout the harvesting process.

Humane harvesting is often done using CO_2 euthanasia. The crickets die quickly and painlessly from carbon dioxide exposure using this method.

CO_2 euthanasia is considered an ethical and humanitarian way of raising insects because it spares the crickets undue agony.

Another gentle method of harvesting crickets is to chill them or utilize refrigeration, which reduces the temperature and puts them into hibernation. By lowering their activity and mobility, the crickets are easier to handle and harvest stress- and injury-free.

Furthermore, by lowering the stress and physical injury to the crickets, using gentle brushes or nets during harvesting can support humane techniques. The welfare of the crickets must come first during the harvesting process if producers are to ensure ethical and sustainable cricket breeding.

Cleaned, Ready, and Packaged Crickets

Crickets must be meticulously cleaned, processed, and packaged after harvesting to be fit for consumption or further use in goods based on crickets.

Cleaning crickets is removing any waste, dung, or uneaten food from their bodies to preserve food safety and cleanliness.

There may be several stages depending on what you want from cricket processing. For example, crickets can be cleaned, roasted, or freeze-dried if they are intended to be eaten straight to enhance their flavor, texture, and shelf life. If, however, the crickets are meant to be used as cricket flour or protein powder, they may be milled, powdered, and sieved to extract the necessary components.

Cricket packaging is still another significant link in the production process. Good packaging keeps crickets fresh, safe, and of excellent quality while they are being delivered. Materials for food-grade packaging must be airtight and bear labels with the product's name, batch number, expiration date, and nutritional value.

Along with whole crickets or processed cricket products, farmers may consider value-added packaging options including meal kits, snack packs, or recipe-ready cricket products to meet consumer tastes and convenience.

All things considered, collecting and processing crickets requires careful planning, observance of moral standards, and food safety. Following best practices in harvesting, processing, and packaging, cricket farmers may create premium cricket products that meet market demands and promote sustainable food systems.

Chapter 7
Marketing And Sales

Any business needs marketing and sales, even cricket farming and cricket product sales. These concepts span a wide range of approaches and strategies intended to identify target customers, create appealing cricket products, and use effective marketing strategies to successfully sell these items.

Identification of the target market is the cornerstone of any successful marketing plan. Farmers of crickets and manufacturers of cricket products must understand their target market. This means looking at the demographics, purchasing patterns, and tastes of potential customers.

Target markets can be extremely varied; they might include foodies interested in other protein sources, athletes, pet owners, and health-conscious consumers. Companies can adapt their offers and marketing plans to meet the needs and interests of these clients using market segmentation and target group identification.

Developing cricket products includes formulating, packaging, and branding techniques. This can mean growing premium crickets for use as human or pet food or as organic fertilizers in agriculture. Protein powders, energy bars, snacks, and even cosmetics are among the products made with crickets.

When creating a product, quality, nutritional value, flavor, texture, and sustainability must all be taken into account. Taking into account ease of use, openness of information, environmental friendliness, and visual appeal, packaging is crucial to attract clients.

Good branding draws attention to how versatile, health-promoting and ecologically friendly cricket goods are.

Increasing brand loyalty, boosting sales, and raising awareness are the goals of the marketing campaigns used to sell crickets and associated goods. Among these strategies could be

Using websites, email marketing, social media, and influencer relationships, digital marketing first and foremost reaches a broad audience and engages with prospective customers.

With blogs, videos, and infographics, content marketing may educate consumers about the benefits of crickets and cricket products while also offering industry news, recipes, and testimonials.

2. Retail Partnerships: To effectively distribute cricket products, dealing with retailers, supermarkets, health food shops, pet stores, and specialized stores.

Creating strong relationships with merchants can lead to better exposure to target customers, opportunities for promotions, and prominent shelf placement.

Three. At trade shows, food expos, health fairs, and neighborhood get-togethers, event marketing involves showcasing cricket products, sampling them, and engaging with consumers directly. These events provide opportunities for participation, networking, and potential partnerships with distributors or wholesalers.

4. Educational Activities: Launching educational activities to raise public awareness of the nutritional value, sustainability, and culinary versatility of crickets. Working with chefs, dietitians, environmentalists, and health organizations can assist in advancing eating insects as a sensible and ecologically friendly option.

5. Using imaginative packaging designs, eco-friendly materials, and instructive labeling, packaging innovation draws consumers in and

communicates key product attributes. Cricket products can be distinguished from traditional offers and, in large part, appeal to consumers who value the environment through the packaging.

6. Sample Programmes: Putting in place sampling programs in stores, at events, or through online sales to allow people to test various items out for themselves. Trial purchases are urged, and sample helps to dispel any early misgivings or misconceptions regarding insect-based food.

7. Use of interactive materials, feedback systems, and loyalty programs to promote customer interaction. Building a fan base for cricket items can lead to referrals, repeat business, and useful data for the next product creation and marketing strategies.

8. Partnerships and Collaborations: Having partnerships with other businesses, organizations, celebrities, or sports teams who are interested in health, sustainability, or fitness concerns could help to increase reach and credibility. Using current

audiences, cobranded initiatives, sponsorships, and cooperative marketing can increase brand exposure.

9. Using press releases, PR campaigns, and media outreach, public relations seeks to get exposure in relevant newspapers, blogs, podcasts, and other media outlets. Good media exposure of the brand can boost consumer confidence in cricket products.

Providing excellent customer service, promptly responding to inquiries, and coming up with practical answers will make customers devoted and trustworthy. Return business is encouraged and the entire customer experience is enhanced by product information, recipe ideas, and instructional materials.

Effective marketing and sales plans for crickets and cricket goods require all things considered, market research, product development, targeted communication, distribution agreements, customer interaction, and ongoing evaluation of consumer preferences and market trends. By adopting a thorough strategy for marketing and sales, businesses associated with cricket may position themselves competitively in the market and benefit from the growing demand for sustainable and healthy food options.

Chapter 8
Standards And Compliance

Entering the world of cricket farming requires knowledge of the legal framework. Among the several aspects of rules and compliance are legal concerns, health and safety standards, certifications, and licensing needs. These elements provide cricket growers with the structure they operate inside, ensuring moral conduct, protecting customers, and environmental sustainability.

Cricket farming is subject to many of the laws and regulations that govern agriculture, animal welfare, food production, and environmental protection. Numerous countries have agricultural practices governed by agricultural laws that specify land use, water use, waste management, and farming activities. Guidelines for cricket housing, feeding, and humane care may also be established by laws controlling animal welfare.

Health and safety laws are much needed in cricket farming to safeguard both workers and consumers. These standards address various subjects, including hygiene practices, equipment safety, pest control methods, and biosecurity protocols. Keeping the environment clean for cricket development and avoiding infection needs adhering to proper hygiene practices.

Techniques for pest management help to control insects that could affect the health of crops and the quantity of crickets. The equipment safety reduces the likelihood of accidents and injuries during farming operations. Making safe cricket products and keeping a healthy farm rely on biosecurity measures that attempt to prevent diseases from being imported and spread among cricket populations.

Licensing and certification are essential elements of regulatory compliance in cricket production. Customers and stakeholders are assured by certifications that specific standards and processes are followed. Common certifications for cricket farming include organic certification, which verifies following organic farming practices and prohibits the use of synthetic pesticides and genetically modified organisms.

Moreover, one may seek certifications in food safety, environmental sustainability, and animal welfare to demonstrate commitment to moral farming practices.

Getting the necessary licenses is another essential part of cricket farming compliance. Depending on the jurisdiction, farmers may have to get licenses for farming, animal care, food production, and business activities. Many times, these licenses demand compliance with certain regulations, such as zoning laws, building codes, and food safety standards.

 A wrong permit might lead to ignorance of the legal consequences and the viability of the cricket farming business.

In cricket farming, regulations, and compliance refer to, to name a few, licensing, certification, and health and safety standards. Following these guidelines ensures moral and ecological behavior, protects the health and safety of staff and consumers, and boosts consumer confidence in cricket products.

By keeping up their knowledge and following legal requirements, cricket farmers can promote high standards of quality and integrity and help the industry grow.

Chapter 9

Troubleshooting And Typical Problems

Success in cricket farming mostly depends on appropriate troubleshooting and resolution of common issues. This covers managing issues with the environment, settling common farming problems, and attending to health issues with crickets. Operating a profitable and healthy cricket farm requires an understanding of these factors.

Managing Health Risks with Crickets

Just a few of the reasons why crickets get sick are diseases, parasites, and starvation. Early detection and management of these issues is necessary to maintain a healthy cricket population.

Worms and mites are two common health issues in crickets. Crickets may become stressed out by these parasites, which would reduce their productivity. Cricket colonies can be routinely checked for parasite infestations and pest control procedures implemented.

Other health concerns are fungal and bacterial infections. They can spread fast on packed cricket fields or in unhygienic conditions. Good hygienic practices, tidy, well-ventilated housing, and routine removal of dead crickets can all prevent infections.

Nutritional deficiencies also impact cricket development and health. It takes providing a balanced diet high in protein, carbohydrates, vitamins, and minerals to encourage healthy growth and reproduction. One can prevent shortages and ensure the greatest possible health for crickets by taking supplements of calcium and other essential minerals.

Handling Environmental Problems

Environment greatly influences cricket farming and can also have an impact on general health and productivity. Maintaining a profitable cricket farm calls for knowledge of and competence with these challenges.

Temperature and relative humidity are two key environmental factors affecting cricket's health and behavior. Crickets thrive in warm, humid conditions even though extreme heat or humidity can stress them out and lead to health problems. By use of suitable ventilation, heating, and cooling systems, the temperature and humidity levels of the cricket habitat must be maintained at the correct range.

Lighting is another aspect of the environment. Nighttime creatures and crickets require a dark environment to survive and breed. Too much light might cause them to feel anxious and to have their natural behavior altered. Drapes or shields that block off light can help give crickets a dark enough home.

The state of the air affects cricket as well. Insufficient ventilation can lead to stagnant air, increased humidity, and the buildup of hazardous gases like ammonia. By putting up suitable ventilation systems and regularly cleaning the cricket habitat, air quality can be increased and healthy cricket growth promoted.

Cricket growers can face several common agricultural problems that require research and solutions in addition to health and environmental ones.

One common issue causing conflict, increased stress, and animosity among crickets is crowding. Preserving ideal stocking densities, and providing enough space, hiding spots, and food and water sources can help to reduce overcrowding issues.

A further challenge is managing waste and odors. Bugs are drawn in by the foul-smelling, buildup of pee and leftover meals. Regular cleaning and waste removal, together with the use of absorbent bedding materials, will help control odor and offer a clean cricket environment.

There are also dietary issues; examples are crickets that show signs of nutritional deficiencies or refuse to eat specific foods. Good eating habits and nutritional imbalances can be corrected by providing a varied diet of fresh fruits and vegetables, calcium supplements, and commercial cricket feed.

Additionally necessary to prevent diseases and pests from entering and multiplying in cricket farms is maintaining biosecurity procedures. This covers setting up cleaning protocols, isolating new cricket supplies, and monitoring for signs of illness or infestation.

Taking everything into account, the best ways to identify and fix common issues in cricket farming are proactive management, regular observation, and prompt reaction. Knowing the factors that impact cricket health and productivity allows farmers to optimize the environment for successful cricket breeding, therefore ensuring a profitable and long-lasting business.

Chapter 10

Advanced Methods And Innovations

Automated farming technologies have completely changed agriculture worldwide, and cricket farming presents a bright new opportunity for the production of environmentally benign insect protein. Modern technology like sensors, robots, and data analytics are combined in these systems to improve every stage of cricket farming, from breeding and feeding to harvesting and processing. One of automated farming's primary advantages in cricket production is its ability to raise output and efficiency while reducing labor costs and environmental impact.

Sensors in automated cricket farming systems enable the monitoring of important factors including te mperature, humidity, pH levels, and feed intake. These sensors are arranged carefully in the cricket farming facility to ensure the ideal growing and development circumstances for the crickets. For example, sensors that track temperature and humidity help crickets grow healthily and lessen stress-related issues. Similar pH sensors ensure the crickets get the optimum possible nutrition and hydration by monitoring the water quality in cricket watering systems.

Robotics is another ground-breaking method for automated cricket farming. Among the various tasks that robotic systems are designed to complete precisely and effectively are harvesting, cleaning, and feeding. Because automatic feeders provide the right amount of food at predefined times, human error is eliminated and the crickets are guaranteed continual nutrition. Cleaning robots maintain hygienic conditions and reduce the risk of disease outbreaks by removing dirt and debris from cricket enclosures. Gathering adult crickets using non-invasive techniques, and harvesting robots reduce suffering and preserve product quality.

Artificial intelligence (AI) and data analytics provide the foundation of modern automated farming systems. By use of massive amounts of data collected from sensors and robotic operations, these technologies enhance production processes. In real-time, AI systems can detect anomalies, predict trends, and adapt to maximize output and make better use of existing resources. Meal patterns can be examined by AI-powered gadgets, for example, for best nutrition and growth. Farmers can adjust production levels as needed by forecasting market demand using patterns in consumption.

The genetic advancement of crickets is another area of innovation with great potential to increase the sustainability and output of cricket farming. Conventional breeding methods have been used to choose desirable traits including growth rate, feed conversion efficiency, and disease resistance. However new prospects for targeted genetic improvement in crickets have been opened up by advances in current genetic technology, most notably CRISPR-Cas9 gene editing.

CRISPR-Cas9 technology allows scientists to precisely modify the cricket DNA to add or delete desired traits. Researchers can enhance cricket nutrition by using genes involved in, for example, protein synthesis, fatty acid composition, or vitamin production.

This genetic advance benefits cricket protein in terms of quality and appeal as a long-term human food supply.

As much as genetic modification, research and development (R&D) advances cricket farming techniques. The main foci of research and development include new feed formulas, housing and infrastructure upgrades, and market and usage research for cricket products. Working together, government, industry, and educational institutions advance innovation and knowledge sharing in cricket farming.

Among the primary R&D domains in cricket farming is sustainable feed development. For crickets, grain, vegetables, and commercial feed formulas are common sources of food. Still, scientists are investigating additional diet components like algae, insect meal from other species, and agricultural waste. Along with reducing production costs, these alternative feeds support the development of a more circular and sustainable farming system.

Projects for research and development in cricket farming also focus on waste and resource management. One can use leftover cricket feed and frass, or insect excrement, as organic fertilizer or animal feed. Applying the concepts of the circular economy, cricket farmers can minimize waste output and maximize resource efficiency, therefore enhancing and maintaining their farming system.

Furthermore, important components of R&D in cricket farming are product development and market research. The food, feed, and pharmaceutical industries are in great need of cricket-based products as consumer interest in alternative proteins grows. R&D programs attempt to create new cricket-based products like protein bars, snacks, pet food, and nutraceuticals by leveraging a range of market niches and value chains.

Finally, research and development, automated farming techniques, and genetic enhancement are driving the growth of cricket farming as a scalable and sustainable source of protein. Using genetics, technology, and scientific understanding, cricket farmers may boost productivity, reduce environmental impact, and meet the growing need for nutrient-dense and environmentally benign protein sources.

Chapter 11
Continued Stories and Case Studies

Case studies and success stories are often useful teaching and motivational tools in many industries, including agriculture. Numerous cricket farming success stories and case studies illustrate the opportunities and challenges faced by farmers and offer perceptive details on the best practices, lessons learned, and inspirational anecdotes for beginners.

Success stories of cricket farmers are presented in the profiles of these farmers. These biographies delve into the background, life lessons discovered, and strategies employed by successful farmers. A profile might, for instance, emphasize a farmer who started small but successfully grew through innovative techniques, marketing strategies, and ecologically responsible practices. These profiles not only recognize accomplishment but also provide future farmers with a route map.

Lessons Learned from Farming Crickets is an anthology of many observations and experiences gathered throughout time. These lessons are frequently drawn from setbacks, mistakes made, and the advancement of farming techniques. For example, farmers might talk about how to control insects, improve feed quality, or make the most of cricket holes. Lessons learned also address topics like financial management, regulatory compliance, and customer engagement, providing a thorough picture of the complexity of the organization.

The best results in cricket farming are captured in tried-and-true methods and techniques. These techniques cover any aspect of farming, from habitat design and maintenance to breeding, feeding, and collecting protocols. Best practices could be, for instance, using sustainable feed sources, maintaining the right temperature and humidity, and using efficient harvesting techniques. Farmers may raise production, reduce costs, and promote environmental sustainability by implementing these best practices.

Inspirational Stories for New Farmers is a collection of inspiring accounts of individuals who firmly and enthusiastically entered the cricket farming industry. Many times, these stories show perseverance in the face of hardship, original approaches to problem-solving, and the transformative impact of cricket farming on family incomes. A motivational narrative might, for example, describe a farmer who, through perseverance and creative problem-solving, surmounted early challenges to succeed and inspire others.

One remarkable cricket farming success story is the experience of small-scale Tennesseean farmer John Smith. John started cricket farming with little money and skeptical neighbors. Even so, his passion for sustainable agriculture and his belief that crickets have enormous promise as a source of protein sustained him. In the beginning, John erected little cricket homes in his garden and carefully monitored the temperature, humidity, and feed quality.

John was becoming more and more knowledgeable and confident. Investing in larger habitats, he improved feed formulations and formed partnerships with local restaurants keen to use cricket flour in their dishes. John became well-known in the farming sector and the media for his innovative approach because of his dedication to environmentally beneficial practices, such as using organic feed and minimizing waste.

Along the way, among other things, John learned the importance of lifelong learning and adaptation. He worked with entomologists, networked with other farmers, and went to seminars to remain up to date on market trends and best techniques. John also welcomed the technology, which he used to automate and streamline his farming processes using data analytics.

The success story of John highlights the value of perseverance, inventiveness, and community support in cricket farming. By showing how sustainable agriculture may not only produce healthy food but also create jobs and promote environmental responsibility, his experience inspires other farmers to enter the field.

Using optimal techniques that increase yield, profitability, and sustainability is another element of cricket farming success. Among such outstanding practices are habitat designs and maintenance. Successful growers prioritize first the construction of perfect cricket habitats, which include areas, humidity, temperature, and ventilation. Natural light, climate control systems, and insulated structures could be used to mimic ideal conditions for cricket growth.

The feeding methods are another crucial part of best practices in cricket farming. Good producers focus on giving their crickets a diet high in nutrients and balanced with supplies of grains, vegetables, and protein. They could also look at cutting-edge feed formulations that contain prebiotics and probiotics for cricket growth and wellness. Sustaining farming heavily relies on efficient feed management, which covers storage, quality control, and cost.

The breeding and harvesting methods are the cornerstone of best practices in cricket farming. Farmers maintain the male-to-female ratios, watch mating behavior, and set up the conditions for egg laying and hatching. Harvesting methods include timely processing for high-quality products, humane methods, and timing according to stages of the cricket life cycle.

Above all technical factors, successful cricket farmers prioritize environmental and ethical sustainability. They might utilize organic and natural materials, reduce their energy and water consumption, and manage their trash by composting or recycling. Among the ethical concerns that support a positive reputation and market acceptance are those of animal welfare, fair labor standards, and open communication with stakeholders.

Among the best cricket-producing methods is a cooperative of farmers in Southeast Asia. To combine their efforts for group success, these farmers formed a group and shared resources, expertise, and market access. They employed integrated methods of pest management, added pet food, fertilizer, and cricket-based snacks to their product range, and engaged consumers through educational campaigns that highlighted the health benefits of eating cricket.

Using implementing best practices and continuous improvement, these farmers enhanced their output and profitability while at the same time advancing environmental protection and community growth. In the cricket farming industry, their success story demonstrates the importance of sustainability, innovation, and collaboration.

Inspirational stories of those who overcame challenges seized opportunities, and bettered their communities are shared with aspiring cricket farmers. One such story tells of Maria Lopez, a former school teacher who now farms crickets in Mexico. It was during a seminar on other protein sources that Maria became interested in crickets.

Despite the first misgivings of her family and friends, Maria pursued her ambition, attending training courses and studying cricket farming techniques.

She started modestly, building a small cricket habitat in her garden and experimenting with different feed mixes. When Maria began selling products produced with crickets to the local markets and saw her cricket population rise, her dedication paid off.

As much as financial success, Maria's story is one of social influence. She battled valiantly to have cricket farming recognized as a healthy and sustainable food source for school meals and community outreach programs. Local government and NGOs helped Maria, and as a result, alliances were created that broadened her impact.

Maria has shown us the need for community service, education, and perseverance in the advancement of alternative farming techniques. Her story inspires incoming farmers to collaborate, think imaginatively, and back ecologically sustainable food systems.

Success stories and case studies in cricket farming, last but not least, offer perceptive details about the workings of the industry, suggested practices, and inspirational individual experiences. Though profiles of successful farmers emphasize a range of strategies and experiences, lessons gained and best practices provide helpful guidance for optimizing farming operations. Amazing stories for would-be farmers show how passion, perseverance, and inventiveness can completely transform agriculture. The cricket farming industry is advanced towards success and sustainability through the rich tapestry of information, motivation, and shared experiences that these stories together create.

Summary

This comprehensive guide to cricket farming has examined every aspect of this innovative and environmentally friendly farming technique. This book, which covers everything from the why and how of growing crickets to handling the difficulties of breeding, harvesting, and selling cricket products, will be highly valuable to both new and experienced farmers.

Over these pages, we have discussed the advantages of cricket farming, including its potential in several markets and its advantages to the environment. We've discussed how to effectively establish a cricket farm, manage the life cycle of the crickets, maximize their food and surroundings, and handle any unforeseen challenges while ensuring that laws and regulations are complied with.

Beyond the basics, this book offers perspectives into innovative techniques, discoveries, and actual success stories. It is a guidebook to help farmers succeed in this exciting and promising field and a monument to the growing importance of insect farming in sustainable agriculture.